BILLY JOEL

T0105966

Cover Photo © Clayton Call / Retna Ltd./MediaPunch

ISBN 978-1-4950-3065-9

HAL•LEONARD®
CORPORATION

7777 W. BLUEMOUND RD. P.O. BOX 13819 MILWAUKEE, WI 53213

In Australia Contact:
Hal Leonard Australia Pty. Ltd.
4 Lentara Court
Cheltenham, Victoria, 3192 Australia
Email: ausadmin@halleonard.com.au

Visit Hal Leonard Online at
www.halleonard.com

AND SO IT GOES

Words and Music by
BILLY JOEL

Moderately slow, freely

HONESTY

Words and Music by
BILLY JOEL

IT'S STILL ROCK AND ROLL TO ME

Words and Music by
BILLY JOEL

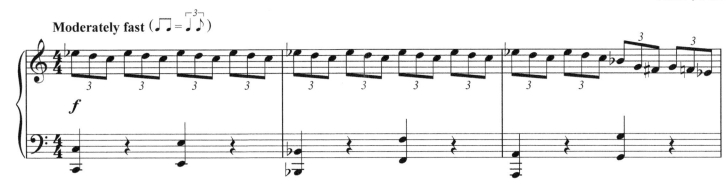

JUST THE WAY YOU ARE

Words and Music by
BILLY JOEL

To Coda ⊕

D.S. al Coda

CODA

rit.

THE LONGEST TIME

Words and Music by
BILLY JOEL

Moderately fast Swing

LULLABYE
(Goodnight, My Angel)

Words and Music by
BILLY JOEL

Ballad, freely

MY LIFE

Words and Music by
BILLY JOEL

Ragtime

To Coda

PIANO MAN

Words and Music by
BILLY JOEL

Moderately fast, straight 8ths

NEW YORK STATE OF MIND

Words and Music by
BILLY JOEL

RIVER OF DREAMS

Words and Music by
BILLY JOEL

SHE'S GOT A WAY

Words and Music by
BILLY JOEL

SHE'S ALWAYS A WOMAN

Words and Music by
BILLY JOEL